CCSS **Genre** Realisti

Essential Quest
What can traditions teach you about
cultures?

A Row of Lamps

by Paul Mason • illustrated by Caroline Hu

Chapter 1
Something Special

))✳((

It was art—my favorite class of the week. Mrs. Jones had asked us to draw something that was really precious to us. I guessed she meant something that was special. I wanted to ask her what she meant but I didn't say anything. I'd only been at school for a few weeks. Being the new kid in class can be difficult. I just put my head down and started drawing.

Mia, the girl sitting next to me, leaned over and stared at the pattern I was drawing. "That's a cool design, Anjali," she said. "I've never seen anything like that before."

I smiled and nodded, but didn't say anything.

"I really like the bright colors and the shapes," said Mia.

"Thanks," I said quietly. "It's called Rangoli. It's a symbol we draw to celebrate Diwali."

"Di-what-i?" Mia asked.

I smiled. "Diwali. It's a festival that happens every year. There are lots of pretty lights and fireworks and good food—plenty of desserts. We always have a party."

"That sounds like fun," Mia laughed. "I like those kinds of parties." She went back to her drawing.

I thought about inviting her over to our house to celebrate the Diwali festival with us. I didn't have any friends in school, and Mia was being kind. But maybe she'd find our Diwali tradition strange, so I didn't ask.

Chapter 2
Light and Dark

⸺⸺⸺) ✸ (⸺⸺⸺

"Dad, would it be OK if I invited Mia over for Diwali?" I asked that night.

"Of course," he said. He was busy getting our Diwali lamps and lanterns ready. I couldn't wait for them to be lit up for the festival.

"But she might think it's strange. She doesn't know anything about Diwali," I said.

Dad stopped what he was doing. "Why do you think we put all these lamps out?"

"To light up the house?" I asked.

Dad smiled. "You're right; it's so that light can beat the dark. But in our culture they're also there to remind us that learning new things is a bit like 'seeing the light.' We believe it brings good luck. Diwali is something everyone can celebrate."

I thought about what Dad said. "So teaching Mia about Diwali would be a good thing?"

"That's right," he said, smiling. "Now the entrance needs to be decorated."

Chapter 3

An Invitation

The next day at school, I still wasn't sure whether to invite Mia. I wanted to go and talk to her at recess, but she was hanging out with a bunch of her friends. I didn't have the courage to ask her in case they all laughed.

So I stayed by myself and ate my snack. Maybe it was better that way.

Later Mia came up to me. "Anjali, I looked up Diwali on the Internet. It means 'row of lamps' right?"

I was surprised. "Yes, we put up lights all around our house. The best part is that Diwali lasts for five days."

"Five whole days?" Mia shook her head. "No way! How come my family doesn't do something like that?"

"You could come over if you like." I was worried she might say no. I didn't want to face disappointment.

But Mia smiled. "Really? I'd love to. But are you sure?"

I nodded quickly. "Sure, Dad said I could invite you over for the main celebration tomorrow night. It'll be fun."

"Great! I'll ask Mom when I get home. There'll be lots of desserts, right?"

"Of course!" I said laughing.

Chapter 4
Looking at the Lights

The next night our house looked beautiful. The lamps on the driveway were golden and glowing. There were lanterns hung everywhere and lights around the windows and doors. The house shone in the dark night. I had made a Rangoli by the front door to welcome everyone.

I kept looking out of the window, waiting for Mia to arrive.

Finally, Mia and her dad walked up the driveway. She ran to greet me. "Happy Diwali," she said.

"You must be Anjali," Mia's dad said. "We've heard all about you." I blushed. "Wow," he said. "Those decorations are beautiful."

We chatted as we walked up to the house. Mia showed her dad the Rangoli I had drawn. I listened with pride as she explained to him what she had learned about Diwali.

I had to smile. Dad was right. Because of me, Mia had learned something new. I had also made a friend. All thanks to Diwali.

Respond to Reading

Summarize

Use details from the story to summarize *A Row of Lamps*. Your graphic organizer may help you.

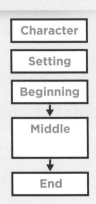

Character

Setting

Beginning
↓
Middle
↓
End

Text Evidence

1. How can you tell that this story is realistic fiction? Which parts are probably true, and which parts are not? Genre

2. What happens when Anjali first meets Mia? Sequence

3. What does *festival* on page 4 mean? Use the clues in the sentence to help you. Sentence Clues

4. Read chapter 3. Write about what happens during recess. Retell the events in order. Write About Reading

Compare Texts
Read about the tradition of Diwali.

Diwali

The festival of Diwali started in India, but today it is celebrated by people around the world. The festival is in the fall and it lasts for up to five days.

Lights are an important part of the holiday. In some parts of India, people float small lamps on the rivers. At night, thousands of small lights drift along the water. In other places, people hang colorful lamps around their homes.

Brijesh Singh/Reuters/CORBIS

Rangoli are drawn, or made from things such as rice, beans, or sand.

Rangoli are another traditional part of Diwali. The patterns are placed in doorways to welcome people. Creating a Rangoli takes time. First, an outline is drawn in rice flour or sand. Then the shape is filled in using colorful sand or spices. Some Rangoli show animals or plants. Others are repeating patterns.

Diwali is a time of fun for everyone. People buy new clothes to wear. They like to give presents to show that they care for one another. There are parties with snacks and desserts.

Laddus are dough balls flavored with almonds.

Make Connections

What traditions are part of the Diwali festival? Essential Question

How did this article help you understand Anjali's culture? Text To Text

Focus on
Social Studies

Purpose To understand the place of traditions in a culture

Procedure

Step 1 ▶ Research Diwali traditions in one region of India.

Step 2 ▶ Write a paragraph about the traditions you learned about.

Step 3 ▶ Share what you learned with others in the class.

Step 4 ▶ Discuss how the Diwali traditions are similar and how they are different in the regions you each researched.